Opposite Tamsin, pattern page 38 this page Zara, pattern page 45, both in Big Wool

Opposite Kyle, pattern page 49, and Patty, pattern page 49, this page Jude, pattern page 32, all in Biggy Print.

Opposite Dylan in Big Wool, pattern page 40, this page Gina in Biggy Print, pattern page 51

This page Guy scarf, pattern page 49, opposite Nik, pattern page 43, both in Big Wool

Gwen, pattern page 44 and Guy scarf, pattern page 49, both in Big Wool

Opposite Tamsin, pattern page 38, this page Jess, pattern page 36, both in Big Wool

This page Gabby, pattern page 46, opposite Lottie, pattern page 41, both in Big Wool

This page Eva in Biggy Print, pattern page 48, opposite Fergus in Big Wool, pattern page 33

Opposite Libby, pattern page 34, this page Stella, pattern page 39, both knitted in Biggy Print and Big Wool

Oppostie Alicia in Big Wool, pattern page 35, this page Mac in Big Wool and Biggy Print, pattern page 30

This page Nik in Big Wool, pattern page 43,
opposite Nat in Big Wool and Biggy Print, pattern page 31

BIGGER PICTURE

Index

Mini in Big Wool, pattern page 46

Mac

Kim Hargreaves

YARN

	XS	S	M	L	XL	
To fit bust	81	86	91	97	102	cm
	32	34	36	38	40	in

Rowan Big Wool and Biggy Print

| A | BW Smoky | 007 | 5 | 5 | 6 | 6 | 7 | x100gm |
| B | BP Thunder | 252 | 2 | 2 | 2 | 2 | 2 | x100gm |

NEEDLES

1 pair 12mm (US 17) needles
1 pair 20mm (US 36) needles

TENSION

8 sts and 12 rows to 10 cm measured over stocking stitch using yarn A and 12mm (US 17) needles.

BACK

Cast on 29 (31: 33: 35: 37) sts using 12mm (US 17) needles and yarn A.
Beg with a K row, cont in st st as folls:
Work 8 rows, ending with a WS row.
Inc 1 st at each end of next and every foll 6th row until there are 35 (37: 39: 41: 43) sts.
Cont straight until back measures 27 (28: 28: 29: 29) cm, ending with a WS row.

Shape armholes

Cast off 2 sts at beg of next 2 rows.
31 (33: 35: 37: 39) sts.
Dec 1 st at each end of next 2 (2: 3: 3: 4) rows.
27 (29: 29: 31: 31) sts.
Cont straight until armhole measures 20 (20: 21: 21: 22) cm, ending with a WS row.

Shape shoulders and back neck

Next row (RS): Cast off 3 sts, K until there are 6 (7: 7: 7: 7) sts on right needle and turn, leaving rem sts on a holder.
Work each side of neck separately.
Cast off 3 sts at beg of next row.
Cast off rem 3 (4: 4: 4: 4) sts.
With RS facing, rejoin yarn to rem sts, cast off centre 9 (9: 9: 11: 11) sts, K to end.
Complete to match first side, reversing shapings.

FRONT

Work as given for back until 6 rows less have been worked than on back to start of shoulder shaping, ending with a WS row.

Shape neck

Next row (RS): K9 (10: 10: 10: 10) and turn, leaving rem sts on a holder.
Work each side of neck separately.
Dec 1 st at neck edge of next 2 rows, then on foll alt row. 6 (7: 7: 7: 7) sts.
Work 1 row, ending with a WS row.

Shape shoulder

Cast off 3 sts at beg of next row.
Work 1 row.
Cast off rem 3 (4: 4: 4: 4) sts.
With RS facing, rejoin yarn to rem sts, cast off centre 9 (9: 9: 11: 11) sts, K to end.
Complete to match first side, reversing shapings.

SLEEVES (both alike)

Cast on 21 (21: 23: 23: 25) sts using 12mm (US 17) needles and yarn A.
Beg with a K row, cont in st st as folls:
Work 14 rows, ending with a WS row.
Inc 1 st at each end of next and every foll 10th row until there are 27 (27: 29: 29: 31) sts.
Cont straight until sleeve measures 45 (45: 46: 46: 46) cm, ending with a WS row.

Shape top

Cast off 2 sts at beg of next 2 rows.
23 (23: 25: 25: 27) sts.
Dec 1 st at each end of next and foll alt row, then on foll 4th row, then on every foll alt row until 11 sts rem, then on foll row, ending with a WS row.
Cast off rem 9 sts.

MAKING UP

PRESS all pieces as described on the information page.
Join right shoulder seam using back stitch, or mattress st if preferred.

Collar

With RS facing, using 20mm (US 36) needles and yarn B, pick up and knit 6 sts down left side of neck, 6 (6: 6: 8: 8) sts from front, 6 sts up right side of neck, then 11 (11: 11: 13: 13) sts from back. 29 (29: 29: 33: 33) sts.
Beg with a K row, work in st st until collar measures 25cm.
Cast off **very loosely**.
See information page for finishing instructions, setting in sleeves using the set-in method.

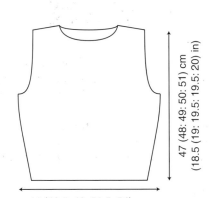

44 (46.5: 49: 51.5: 54) cm
(17.5 (18.5: 19.5: 20.5: 21.5) in)

47 (48: 49: 50: 51) cm
(18.5 (19: 19.5: 19.5: 20) in)

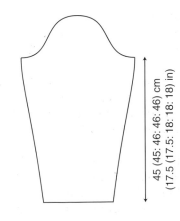

45 (45: 46: 46: 46) cm
(17.5 (17.5: 18: 18: 18) in)

DESIGN NUMBER 2

NAT

KIM HARGREAVES

YARN

	XS	S	M	L	XL
To fit bust	81	86	91	97	102 cm
	32	34	36	38	40 in

Rowan Big Wool and Biggy Print

| A | BW | Shocking | 009 | 3 | 3 | 4 | 4 | 5 | x100gm |
| B | BP | Allsorts | 255 | 2 | 2 | 2 | 2 | 2 | x100gm |

NEEDLES

1 pair 12mm (US 17) needles
1 pair 20mm (US 36) needles

TENSION

8 sts and 12 rows to 10 cm measured over stocking stitch using yarn A and 12mm (US 17) needles.

Pattern note: As row end edges form actual finished armhole edges of garment, it is important these edges are kept neat. Therefore avoid joining in new balls of yarn at these edges.

BACK

Cast on 33 (35: 37: 39: 41) sts using 12mm (US 17) needles and yarn A.
Beg with a K row, cont in st st as folls:
Work 6 rows, ending with a WS row.

Dec 1 st at each end of next and every foll 4th row until 27 (29: 31: 33: 35) sts rem.
Work 5 rows.
Inc 1 st at each end of next and every foll 6th row until there are 33 (35: 37: 39: 41) sts.
Cont straight until back measures 37 (38: 38: 39: 39) cm, ending with a WS row.

Shape armholes

Cast off 3 sts at beg of next 2 rows.
27 (29: 31: 33: 35) sts.
Next row (RS): K2, K2tog, K to last 4 sts, K2tog tbl, K1, pick up loop lying between needles and place loop on right needle (**note**: this loop does NOT count as a st), sl last st knitwise.
Row 2: P tog first st and the loop, P1, P2tog tbl, P to last 4 sts, P2tog, P1, pick up loop lying between needles and place loop on right needle (**note**: this loop does NOT count as a st), sl last st purlwise.
Row 3: K tog tbl first st and the loop, (K1, K2tog) 0 (0: 1: 1: 1) times, K to last 1 (1: 4: 4: 4) sts, (K2tog tbl, K1) 0 (0: 1: 1: 1) times, pick up loop lying between needles and place loop on right needle, sl last st knitwise.
Row 4: P tog first st and the loop, (P1, P2tog tbl) 0 (0: 0: 0: 1) times, P to last 1 (1: 1: 1: 4) sts, (P2tog, P1) 0 (0: 0: 0: 1) times, pick up loop lying between needles and place loop on right needle, sl last st purlwise.
23 (25: 25: 27: 27) sts.
Last 2 rows set the armhole slip st edging and st st.
Keeping slip st armhole edging correct as set, cont as folls:
Cont straight until armhole measures 18 (18: 19: 19: 20) cm, ending with a WS row.

Shape shoulders and back neck

Next row (RS): Cast off 2 (3: 3: 3: 3) sts, K until there are 6 sts on right needle and turn, leaving rem sts on a holder.
Work each side of neck separately.
Cast off 3 sts at beg of next row.
Cast off rem 3 sts.
With RS facing, rejoin yarn to rem sts, cast off centre 7 (7: 7: 9: 9) sts, patt to end.
Complete to match first side, reversing shapings.

FRONT

Work as given for back until 6 rows less have been worked than on back to start of shoulder shaping, ending with a WS row.

Shape neck

Keeping slip st armhole edging correct as set, cont as folls:
Next row (RS): Patt 8 (9: 9: 9: 9) sts and turn, leaving rem sts on a holder.
Work each side of neck separately.
Dec 1 st at neck edge of next 2 rows, then on foll alt row. 5 (6: 6: 6: 6) sts.
Work 1 row, ending with a WS row.

Shape shoulder

Cast off 2 (3: 3: 3: 3) sts at beg of next row.
Work 1 row.
Cast off rem 3 sts.
With RS facing, rejoin yarn to rem sts, cast off centre 7 (7: 7: 9: 9) sts, patt to end.
Complete to match first side, reversing shapings.

MAKING UP

PRESS all pieces as described on the information page.
Join right shoulder seam using back stitch, or mattress st if preferred.

Collar

With RS facing, using 20mm (US 36) needles and yarn B, pick up and knit 6 sts down left side of neck, 6 (6: 6: 8: 8) sts from front, 6 sts up right side of neck, then 10 (10: 10: 12: 12) sts from back. 28 (28: 28: 32: 32) sts.
Beg with a K row, work in st st until collar measures 23cm.
Cast off **very loosely**.
See information page for finishing instructions, reversing collar seam for turn-back.

55 (56: 57: 58: 59) cm
(21.5 (22: 22.5: 23: 23) in)

41.5 (44: 46.5: 49: 51.5) cm
(16.5 (17.5: 18.5: 19.5: 20.5) in)

DESIGN NUMBER 3

JUDE

KIM HARGREAVES

YARN

	XS	S	M	L	XL	
To fit bust 81	86	91	97	102	cm
	32	34	36	38	40	in

Rowan Biggy Print

| | 9 | 10 | 11 | 12 | 13 | x100gm |

(photographed in Glum 244)

NEEDLES

1 pair 20mm (US 36) needles

TENSION

5½ sts and 7 rows to 10 cm measured over
stocking stitch using 20mm (US 36) needles.

BACK

Cast on 23 (25: 27: 29: 31) sts using 20mm
(US 36) needles.
Beg with a K row, cont in st st as folls:
Work 4 rows, ending with a WS row.
Dec 1 st at each end of next and foll 4th row.
19 (21: 23: 25: 27) sts.
Work 3 rows.
Inc 1 st at each end of next and foll 4th row.
23 (25: 27: 29: 31) sts.
Cont straight until back measures 29 (30: 30: 31:
31) cm, ending with a WS row.

Shape armholes

Cast off 2 sts at beg of next 2 rows.
19 (21: 23: 25: 27) sts.
Dec 1 st at each end of next 1 (2: 2: 3: 3) rows.
17 (17: 19: 19: 21) sts.
Cont straight until armhole measures 20 (20: 21:
21: 22) cm, ending with a WS row.

Shape shoulders and back neck

Next row (RS): Cast off 2 sts, K until there are
4 (4: 5: 4: 5) sts on right needle and turn, leaving
rem sts on a holder.
Work each side of neck separately.
Cast off 2 sts at beg of next row.
Cast off rem 2 (2: 3: 2: 3) sts.
With RS facing, rejoin yarn to rem sts, cast off
centre 5 (5: 5: 7: 7) sts, K to end.
Complete to match first side, reversing shapings.

FRONT

Work as given for back until 4 rows less have
been worked than on back to start of shoulder
shaping, ending with a WS row.

Shape neck

Next row (RS): K6 (6: 7: 6: 7) and turn,
leaving rem sts on a holder.
Work each side of neck separately.
Dec 1 st at neck edge of next 2 rows.
4 (4: 5: 4: 5) sts.
Work 1 row, ending with a WS row.

Shape shoulder

Cast off 2 sts at beg of next row.
Work 1 row.
Cast off rem 2 (2: 3: 2: 3) sts.
With RS facing, rejoin yarn to rem sts, cast off
centre 5 (5: 5: 7: 7) sts, K to end.
Complete to match first side, reversing shapings.

SLEEVES (both alike)

Cast on 17 (17: 19: 19: 19) sts using 20mm
(US 36) needles.
Beg with a K row, cont in st st as folls:
Work 18 (18: 18: 18: 10) rows, ending with a
WS row.
Inc 1 st at each end of next and every foll - (-: -:
-: 10th) row. 19 (19: 21: 21: 23) sts.
Cont straight until sleeve measures 46 (46:
47: 47: 47) cm from markers, ending with a
WS row.

Shape top

Cast off 2 sts at beg of next 2 rows.
15 (15: 17: 17: 19) sts.

Dec 1 st at each end of next and foll 4th row,
then on every foll alt row until 9 sts rem, then
on foll row, ending with a WS row.
Cast off rem 7 sts.

MAKING UP

PRESS all pieces as described on the
information page.
Join right shoulder seam using back stitch, or
mattress st if preferred.

Collar

With RS facing and using 20mm (US 36)
needles, pick up and knit 6 sts down left side of
neck, 5 (5: 5: 7: 7) sts from front, 6 sts up right
side of neck, then 9 (9: 9: 11: 11) sts from back.
26 (26: 26: 30: 30) sts.
Beg with a K row, work in st st until collar
measures 27cm.
Cast off very loosely.
See information page for finishing instructions,
setting in sleeves using the set-in method.

49 (50: 51: 52: 53) cm
(19.5 (19.5: 20: 20.5: 21) in)

42 (45.5: 49: 52.5: 56.5) cm
(16.5 (18: 19.5: 20.5: 22) in)

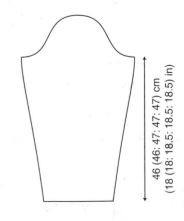

46 (46: 47: 47: 47) cm
(18 (18: 18.5: 18.5: 18.5) in)

FERGUS

KIM HARGREAVES

YARN

	ladies			mens	
	S	M	L	M	L	XL
To fit bust 86	91	97	102	107	112 cm
34	36	38	40	42	44 in

Rowan Big Wool

8 8 9 9 10 11 x 100gm

(photographed in Sugar Spun 016)

NEEDLES

1 pair 12mm (US 17) needles

TENSION

8 sts and 12 rows to 10 cm measured over stocking stitch using 12mm (US 17) needles.

Pattern note: The pattern is written for the 3 ladies sizes, followed by the mens sizes in **bold**. Where only one figure appears this applies to all sizes in that group.

BACK

Cast on 44 (46: 48: **50: 52: 54**) sts using 12mm (US 17) needles.
Row 1 (RS): P0 (**1: 0: 0**), K1 (2: 3: **3: 0: 1**), ★P2, K3, rep from ★ to last 3 (4: 0: **1: 2: 3**) sts, P2 (2: 0: **1: 2: 2**), K1 (2: 0: **0: 0: 1**).

Row 2: K0 (**1: 0: 0**), P1 (2: 3: **3: 0: 1**), ★K2, P3, rep from ★ to last 3 (4: 0: **1: 2: 3**) sts, K2 (2: 0: **1: 2: 2**), P1 (2: 0: **0: 0: 1**).
These 2 rows form rib.
Work in rib for a further 6 rows, ending with a WS row.
Beg with a K row, cont in st st as folls:
Work straight until back measures 36 (**38**) cm, ending with a WS row.
Shape armholes
Cast off 3 sts at beg of next 2 rows.
38 (40: 42: **44: 46: 48**) sts.
Dec 1 st at each end of next 3 rows.
32 (34: 36: **38: 40: 42**) sts.
Cont straight until armhole measures 25 (26: 27: **28: 29: 30**) cm, ending with a WS row.
Shape shoulders and back neck
Cast off 3 (**4**) sts at beg of next 2 rows.
26 (28: 30: **30: 32: 34**) sts.
Next row (RS): Cast off 3 (**4**) sts, K until there are 6 (7: 7: **6: 6: 7**) sts on right needle and turn, leaving rem sts on a holder.
Work each side of neck separately.
Cast off 3 sts at beg of next row.
Cast off rem 3 (4: 4: **3: 3: 4**) sts.
With RS facing, rejoin yarn to rem sts, cast off centre 8 (8: 10: **10: 12: 12**) sts, K to end.
Complete to match first side, reversing shapings.

FRONT

Work as given for back until 6 (**8**) rows less have been worked than on back to start of shoulder shaping, ending with a WS row.
Shape neck
Next row (RS): K13 (14: 14: **16: 16: 17**) and turn, leaving rem sts on a holder.
Work each side of neck separately.
Dec 1 st at neck edge of next 4 rows, then on foll 0 (**1**) alt row. 9 (10: 10: **11: 11: 12**) sts.
Work 1 row, ending with a WS row.
Shape shoulder
Cast off 3 (**4**) sts at beg of next and foll alt row.
Work 1 row.
Cast off rem 3 (4: 4: **3: 3: 4**) sts.
With RS facing, rejoin yarn to rem sts, cast off centre 6 (6: 8: **6: 8: 8**) sts, K to end.
Complete to match first side, reversing shapings.

SLEEVES (both alike)

Cast on 24 (24: 26: **26: 28: 28**) sts using 12mm (US 17) needles.

Row 1 (RS): K1 (1: 2: **2: 3: 3**), ★P2, K3, rep from ★ to last 3 (3: 4: **4: 5: 5**) sts, P2, K1 (1: 2: **2: 3: 3**).
Row 2: P1 (1: 2: **2: 3: 3**), ★K2, P3, rep from ★ to last 3 (3: 4: **4: 5: 5**) sts, K2, P1 (1: 2: **2: 3: 3**).
These 2 rows form rib.
Work in rib for a further 6 rows, ending with a WS row.
Beg with a K row, cont in st st as folls:
Inc 1 st at each end of 5th and every foll 6th row to 36 (34: 38: **36: 38: 36**) sts, then on every foll 4th row until there are 38 (40: 42: **44: 46: 48**) sts.
Cont straight until sleeve measures 46 (47: 48: **50: 51: 52**) cm, ending with a WS row.
Shape top
Cast off 3 sts at beg of next 2 rows.
32 (34: 36: **38: 40: 42**) sts.
Dec 1 st at each end of next and foll 2 alt rows.
Work 1 row, ending with a WS row.
Cast off rem 26 (28: 30: **32: 34: 36**) sts.

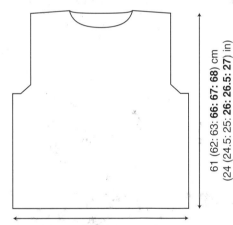

61 (62: 63: **66: 67: 68**) cm
(24 (24.5: 25: **26: 26.5: 27**) in)

55 (57.5: 60: **62.5: 65: 67.5**) cm
(21.5 (22.5: 23.5: **24.5: 25.5: 26.5**) in)

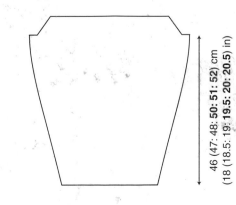

46 (47: 48: **50: 51: 52**) cm
(18 (18.5: 19: **19.5: 20: 20.5**) in)

pick up and knit 10 (**12**) sts down left side of
neck, 6 (6: 8: **6: 8: 8**) sts from front,
10 (**12**) sts up right side of neck, then 14 (14: 17:
15: 18: 18) sts from back.
40 (40: 45: **45: 50: 50**) sts.
Row 1 (WS): *P2, K3, rep from * to end.

Row 2: *P3, K2, rep from * to end.
Rep last 2 rows until collar measures 24cm.
Cast off **very loosely**.
See information page for finishing instructions,
setting in sleeves using the shallow set-in
method and reversing collar seam for turn-back.

Design number 5

LIBBY

KIM HARGREAVES

YARN

	XS	S	M	L	XL	
To fit bust	81	86	91	97	102	cm
	32	34	36	38	40	in

Rowan Biggy Print and Big Wool

| A | BP | Humbug | 254 | 6 | 6 | 7 | 8 | 8 | x 100gm |
| B | BW | Smoky | 007 | 2 | 2 | 2 | 2 | 2 | x 100gm |

NEEDLES

1 pair 12mm (US 17) needles
1 pair 20mm (US 36) needles

TENSION

5½ sts and 7 rows to 10 cm measured over
stocking stitch using 20mm (US 36) needles.

BACK

Cast on 18 (20: 22: 24: 26) sts using 20mm
(US 36) needles and yarn A.
Beg with a K row, cont in st st as folls:
Work 8 rows, ending with a WS row.
Inc 1 st at each end of next and foll 6th row.
22 (24: 26: 28: 30) sts.
Cont straight until back measures 27 (28: 28: 29:
29) cm, ending with a WS row.
Shape armholes
Cast off 2 sts at beg of next 2 rows.
18 (20: 22: 24: 26) sts.
Dec 1 st at each end of next 1 (1: 2: 2: 3) rows.
16 (18: 18: 20: 20) sts.
Cont straight until armhole measures 20 (20: 21:
21: 22) cm, ending with a WS row.
Shape shoulders and back neck
Next row (RS): Cast off 2 sts, K until there are
4 sts on right needle and turn, leaving rem sts on
a holder.
Work each side of neck separately.
Cast off 2 sts at beg of next row.
Cast off rem 2 sts.
With RS facing, rejoin yarn to rem sts, cast off
centre 4 (6: 6: 8: 8) sts, K to end.
Complete to match first side, reversing shapings.

FRONT

Work as given for back until 4 rows less have
been worked than on back to start of shoulder
shaping, ending with a WS row.
Shape neck
Next row (RS): K6 and turn, leaving rem sts
on a holder.
Work each side of neck separately.
Dec 1 st at neck edge of next 2 rows. 4 sts.
Work 1 row, ending with a WS row.
Shape shoulder
Cast off 2 sts at beg of next row.

Work 1 row.
Cast off rem 2 sts.
With RS facing, rejoin yarn to rem sts, cast off
centre 4 (6: 6: 8: 8) sts, K to end.
Complete to match first side, reversing shapings.

MAKING UP

PRESS all pieces as described on the
information page.
Join right shoulder seam using back stitch, or
mattress st if preferred.
Collar
With RS facing, using 12mm (US 17) needles
and yarn B, pick up and knit 8 sts down left side
of neck, 7 (9: 9: 11: 11) sts from front, 8 sts up
right side of neck, then 12 (14: 14: 16: 16) sts
from back. 35 (39: 39: 43: 43) sts.
Beg with a P row, work in rev st st until collar
measures 30cm.
Cast off very loosely.
See information page for finishing instructions,
reversing collar seam for turn-back.

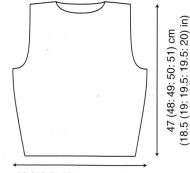

40 (43.5: 47.5: 51: 54.5) cm
(15.5 (17: 18.5: 20: 21.5) in)

47 (48: 49: 50: 51) cm
(18.5 (19: 19.5: 19.5: 20) in)

ALICIA

KIM HARGREAVES

YARN

	XS	S	M	L	XL	
To fit bust	81	86	91	97	102	cm
	32	34	36	38	40	in

Rowan Big Wool

| | 6 | 6 | 7 | 7 | 8 | x100gm |

(photographed in Pip 015)

NEEDLES

1 pair 12mm (US 17) needles

ZIP

Open-ended zip to fit

TENSION

8 sts and 12 rows to 10 cm measured over moss stitch using 12mm (US 17) needles.

BACK

Cast on 31 (33: 35: 37: 39) sts using 12mm (US 17) needles.
Purl 8 rows, ending with a WS row.
Cont in moss st as folls:
Row 1 (RS): P1 (0: 1: 0: 1), ★K1, P1, rep from ★ to last 0 (1: 0: 1: 0) st, K0 (1: 0: 1: 0).
Row 2: As row 1.
These 2 rows form moss st.

Cont in moss st, inc 1 st at each end of next and foll 10th row. 35 (37: 39: 41: 43) sts.
Cont straight until back measures 30 (31: 31: 32: 32) cm, ending with a WS row.
Shape armholes
Keeping moss st correct, cast off 2 sts at beg of next 2 rows. 31 (33: 35: 37: 39) sts.
Dec 1 st at each end of next 2 (2: 3: 3: 4) rows. 27 (29: 29: 31: 31) sts.
Cont straight until armhole measures 20 (20: 21: 21: 22) cm, ending with a WS row.
Shape shoulders and back neck
Next row (RS): Cast off 4 sts, moss st until there are 7 (8: 8: 8: 8) sts on right needle and turn, leaving rem sts on a holder.
Work each side of neck separately.
Cast off 3 sts at beg of next row.
Cast off rem 4 (5: 5: 5: 5) sts.
With RS facing, rejoin yarn to rem sts, cast off centre 5 (5: 5: 7: 7) sts, moss st to end.
Complete to match first side, reversing shapings.

LEFT FRONT
Cast on 16 (17: 18: 19: 20) sts using 12mm (US 17) needles.
Purl 8 rows, ending with a WS row.
Cont as folls:
Row 1 (RS): P1 (0: 1: 0: 1), ★K1, P1, rep from ★ to last st, P1.
Row 2: P1, ★P1, K1, rep from ★ to last 1 (0: 1: 0: 1) st, P1 (0: 1: 0: 1).
These 2 rows set the sts – front opening edge 2 sts worked as P sts on every row with all other sts in moss st.
Cont as set, inc 1 st at beg of next and foll 10th row. 18 (19: 20: 21: 22) sts.
Cont straight until left front matches back to beg of armhole shaping, ending with a WS row.
Shape armhole
Keeping moss st correct, cast off 2 sts at beg of next row. 16 (17: 18: 19: 20) sts.
Work 1 row.
Dec 1 st at armhole edge of next 2 (2: 3: 3: 4) rows. 14 (15: 15: 16: 16) sts.
Cont straight until 7 (7: 7: 9: 9) rows less have been worked than on back to start of shoulder shaping, ending with a RS row.
Shape neck
Next row (WS): P2, K1, P1 and slip these 4 sts onto a holder, moss st to end.
10 (11: 11: 12: 12) sts.

Dec 1 st at neck edge of next and foll 1 (1: 1: 2: 2) alt rows. 8 (9: 9: 9: 9) sts.
Work 3 rows, ending with a WS row.
Shape shoulder
Cast off 4 sts at beg of next row.
Work 1 row.
Cast off rem 4 (5: 5: 5: 5) sts.

RIGHT FRONT
Cast on 16 (17: 18: 19: 20) sts using 12mm (US 17) needles.
Purl 8 rows, ending with a WS row.
Cont as folls:
Row 1 (RS): P1, ★P1, K1, rep from ★ to last 1 (0: 1: 0: 1) st, P1 (0: 1: 0: 1).

50 (51: 52: 53: 54) cm
(19.5 (20: 20.5: 21: 21.5) in)

44 (46.5: 49: 51.5: 54) cm
(17.5 (18.5: 19.5: 20.5: 21.5) in)

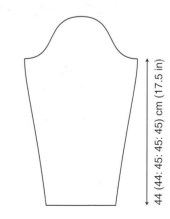

44 (44: 45: 45: 45) cm (17.5 in)

Row 2: P1 (0: 1: 0: 1), *K1, P1, rep from * to last st, P1.

These 2 rows set the sts – front opening edge 2 sts worked as P sts on every row with all other sts in moss st.

Cont as set, inc 1 st at end of next and foll 10th row. 18 (19: 20: 21: 22) sts.

Complete to match left front, reversing shapings.

SLEEVES (both alike)

Cast on 19 (21: 21: 23: 23) sts using 12mm (US 17) needles.

Purl 10 rows, ending with a WS row.

Cont in moss st as folls:

Row 1 (RS): K1, *P1, K1, rep from * to end.

Row 2: As row 1.

These 2 rows form moss st.

Cont in moss st, inc 1 st at each end of next and every foll 14th (20th: 14th: 20th: 14th) row until there are 25 (25: 27: 27: 29) sts.

Cont straight until sleeve measures 44 (44: 45: 45: 45) cm, ending with a WS row.

Shape top

Keeping moss st correct, cast off 2 sts at beg of next 2 rows. 21 (21: 23: 23: 25) sts.

Dec 1 st at each end of next and foll alt row, then on every foll 4th row until 13 (13: 15: 15: 17) sts rem.

Work 1 row, ending with a WS row.

Dec 1 st at each end of next and foll 0 (0: 1: 1: 2) alt rows, then on foll row, ending with a WS row.

Cast off rem 9 sts.

MAKING UP

PRESS all pieces as described on the info page. Join both shoulder seams using back stitch, or mattress st if preferred.

Collar

With RS facing and using 12mm (US 17) needles, slip 4 sts from right front holder onto right needle, rejoin yarn and pick up and knit 8 (8: 8: 10: 10) sts up right side of neck, 10 (10: 10: 12: 12) sts from back, and 8 (8: 8: 10: 10) sts down left side of neck, then patt 4 sts from left front holder. 34 (34: 34: 40: 40) sts.

Knit 8 rows.

Cast off knitwise **very loosely** (on WS).

See information page for finishing instructions, setting in sleeves using the set-in method. Insert zip into front opening.

JESS

KIM HARGREAVES

YARN

	XS	S	M	L	XL	
To fit bust	81	86	91	97	102	cm
	32	34	36	38	40	in

Rowan Big Wool

| | 6 | 7 | 8 | 8 | 9 | x100gm |

(photographed in Whoosh 014)

NEEDLES

1 pair 12mm (US 17) needles
Cable needle

BUTTONS – 8 x 75326

TENSION

8 sts and 12 rows to 10 cm measured over moss stitch using 12mm (US 17) needles.

SPECIAL ABBREVIATIONS

C4B = Cable 4 back Slip next 2 sts onto cn and leave at back of work, K2, then K2 from cn.
C4F = Cable 4 front Slip next 2 sts onto cn and leave at front of work, K2, then K2 from cn.

BACK

Cast on 34 (36: 38: 40: 42) sts using 12mm (US 17) needles.

Row 1 (RS): P0 (1: 0: 0: 0), K2 (2: 0: 1: 2), *P2, K2, rep from * to last 0 (1: 2: 3: 0) sts, P0 (1: 2: 2: 0), K0 (0: 0: 1: 0).

Row 2: K0 (1: 0: 0: 0), P2 (2: 0: 1: 2), *K2, P2, rep from * to last 0 (1: 2: 3: 0) sts, K0 (1: 2: 2: 0), P0 (0: 0: 1: 0).

These 2 rows form rib.

Work in rib for a further 4 rows, ending with a WS row. Beg with a K row, work in st st as folls:

Work 4 rows.

Dec 1 st at each end of next and every foll 4th row until 28 (30: 32: 34: 36) sts rem.

Work 5 rows, ending with a WS row.

Inc 1 st at each end of next and every foll 6th row until there are 34 (36: 38: 40: 42) sts.

Cont straight until back measures 35 (36: 36: 37: 37) cm, ending with a WS row.

Shape armholes

Cast off 3 sts at beg of next 2 rows.

28 (30: 32: 34: 36) sts.

Dec 1 st at each end of next 2 (2: 3: 3: 4) rows.

24 (26: 26: 28: 28) sts.

Cont straight until armhole measures 20 (20: 21: 21: 22) cm, ending with a WS row.

Shape shoulders and back neck

Next row (RS): Cast off 3 sts, K until there are 6 (7: 7: 7: 7) sts on right needle and turn, leaving rem sts on a holder.

Work each side of neck separately.

Cast off 3 sts at beg of next row.

Cast off rem 3 (4: 4: 4: 4) sts.

With RS facing, rejoin yarn to rem sts, cast off centre 6 (6: 6: 8: 8) sts, K to end.

Complete to match first side, reversing shapings.

LEFT FRONT

Cast on 22 (23: 24: 25: 26) sts using 12mm (US 17) needles.

Row 1 (RS): K0 (0: 1: 0: 0), P1 (2: 2: 0: 1), (K2, P2) 2 (2: 2: 3: 3) times, K4, P2, K2, (P1, K1) twice, P1.

Row 2: (P1, K1) twice, P3, K2, P4, (K2, P2) 2 (2: 2: 3: 3) times, K1 (2: 2: 0: 1), P0 (0: 1: 0: 0).

Rep last 2 rows twice more.

Cont in patt as folls:

Row 1 (RS): K to last 15 sts, P2, C4B, P2, K2, (P1, K1) twice, P1.

Row 2 and every foll alt row: (P1, K1) twice, P3, K2, P4, K2, P to end.

Row 3: K to last 15 sts, P2, K4, P2, K2, (P1, K1) twice, P1.

Row 5: K2tog, K to last 15 sts, P2, K4, P2, K2, (P1, K1) twice, P1. 21 (22: 23: 24: 25) sts.
Row 7: K to last 15 sts, P2, C4F, P2, K2, (P1, K1) twice, P1.
Row 9: As row 5. 20 (21: 22: 23: 24) sts.
Row 11: As row 3.
Row 12: As row 2.
These 12 rows form patt and start side seam shaping.
Keeping patt correct, cont as folls:
Dec 1 st at beg of next row.
19 (20: 21: 22: 23) sts.
Work 5 rows, ending with a WS row.
Inc 1 st at beg of next and every foll 6th row until there are 22 (23: 24: 25: 26) sts.
Cont straight until left front matches back to beg of armhole shaping, ending with a WS row.

Shape armhole
Cast off 3 sts at beg of next row.
19 (20: 21: 22: 23) sts.
Work 1 row.
Dec 1 st at armhole edge of next 2 (2: 3: 3: 4) rows.
17 (18: 18: 19: 19) sts.
Cont straight until 9 rows less have been worked than on back to start of shoulder shaping, ending with a RS row.

Shape neck
Next row (WS): Patt 8 (8: 8: 9: 9) sts and slip these sts onto a holder, patt to end.
9 (10: 10: 10: 10) sts.
Dec 1 st at neck edge of next and foll 2 alt rows.
6 (7: 7: 7: 7) sts.
Work 3 rows, ending with a WS row.

Shape shoulder
Cast off 3 sts at beg of next row.
Work 1 row. Cast off rem 3 (4: 4: 4: 4) sts.
Mark positions for 6 buttons along front opening edge – first to come in row 13, last to come just below neck shaping and rem 4 buttons evenly spaced between.

RIGHT FRONT
Cast on 22 (23: 24: 25: 26) sts using 12mm (US 17) needles.
Row 1 (RS): (P1, K1) twice, P1, K2, P2, K4, (P2, K2) 2 (2: 2: 3: 3) times, P1 (2: 2: 0: 1), K0 (0: 1: 0: 0).
Row 2: P0 (0: 1: 0: 0), K1 (2: 2: 0: 1), (P2, K2) 2 (2: 2: 3: 3) times, P4, K2, P3, (K1, P1) twice.
Rep last 2 rows twice more.
Cont in patt as folls:

Row 1 (RS): (P1, K1) twice, P1, K2, P2, C4F, P2, K to end.
Row 2 and every foll alt row: P to last 15 sts, K2, P4, K2, P3, (K1, P1) twice.
Row 3: (P1, K1) twice, P1, K2, P2, K4, P2, K to end.
Row 5: (P1, K1) twice, P1, K2, P2, K4, P2, K to last 2 sts, K2tog. 21 (22: 23: 24: 25) sts.
Row 7 (buttonhole row): P1, K2tog, yfwd (to make first buttonhole), K1, P1, K2, P2, C4B, P2, K to end.
Row 9: As row 5. 20 (21: 22: 23: 24) sts.
Row 11: As row 3.
Row 12: As row 2.
These 12 rows form patt and start side seam shaping.
Keeping patt correct and working a further 5 buttonholes to correspond with positions marked for buttons, complete to match left front, reversing shapings.

SLEEVES (both alike)
Cast on 18 (20: 20: 22: 22) sts using 12mm (US 17) needles.
Row 1 (RS): P0 (1: 1: 2: 2), ★K2, P2, rep from ★ to last 2 (3: 3: 0: 0) sts, K2 (2: 2: 0: 0), P0 (1: 1: 0: 0).
Row 2: K0 (1: 1: 2: 2), ★P2, K2, rep from ★ to last 2 (3: 3: 0: 0) sts, P2 (2: 2: 0: 0), K0 (1: 1: 0: 0).
These 2 rows form rib.
Work in rib for a further 4 rows, end with a WS row.
Beg with a K row, cont in st st, inc 1 st at each end of 7th and every foll 10th (16th: 10th: 16th: 10th) row until there are 26 (26: 28: 28: 30) sts.
Cont straight until sleeve measures 45 (45: 46: 46: 46) cm, ending with a WS row.

Shape top
Cast off 3 sts at beg of next 2 rows.
20 (20: 22: 22: 24) sts.
Dec 1 st at each end of next and foll alt row, then on every foll 4th row until 12 (12: 14: 14: 16) sts rem.
Work 1 row, ending with a WS row.
Dec 1 st at each end of next and foll 0 (0: 1: 1: 2) alt rows, then on foll row, ending with a WS row.
Cast off rem 8 sts.

MAKING UP
PRESS all pieces as described on the info page.
Join both shoulder seams using back stitch, or mattress st if preferred.

Collar
With RS facing and using 12mm (US 17) needles, slip 8 (8: 8: 9: 9) sts from right front holder onto right needle, rejoin yarn and pick up and knit 10 sts up right side of neck, 12 (12: 12: 14: 14) sts from back, and 10 sts down left side of neck, then patt 8 (8: 8: 9: 9) sts from left front holder. 48 (48: 48: 52: 52) sts.
Row 1 (WS): Moss st 5 sts, P2, ★K2, P2, rep from ★ to last 5 sts, moss st to end.
Row 2: Moss st 5 sts, K2, ★P2, K2, rep from ★ to last 5 sts, moss st to end.
These 2 rows set the sts – front opening edge 5 sts in moss st with all other sts in rib.
Cont as set for 1 row more, end with a WS row.
Row 4 (RS): P1, K2tog, yfwd (to make 7th buttonhole), K1, P1, patt to end.
Work 7 rows.
Row 12: As row 4.
Work a further 2 rows.
Cast off in patt very loosely (on WS).
See information page for finishing instructions, setting in sleeves using the set-in method.

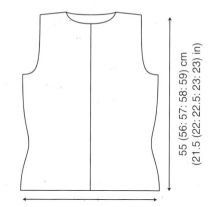

42.5 (45: 47.5: 50: 52.5) cm
(16.5 (17.5: 18.5: 19.5: 20.5) in)

55 (56: 57: 58: 59) cm
(22: 22.5: 23: 23) in)

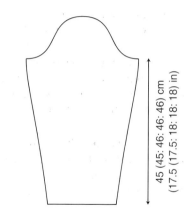

45 (45: 46: 46: 46) cm
(17.5: 18: 18: 18) in)

TAMSIN

KIM HARGREAVES

YARN

	XS	S	M	L	XL	
To fit bust	81	86	91	97	102	cm
	32	34	36	38	40	in

Rowan Big Wool

Long two-colour sweater

A Stormy	011	5	5	6	6	7	x 100gm
B Arctic	013	4	4	4	5	5	x 100gm

Short multi-colour sweater

A Sherbet Lime	002	2	2	3	3	3	x 100gm
B Shocking	009	2	2	2	3	3	x 100gm
C Smitten Kitten	003	3	3	3	3	3	x 100gm
D Whoosh	014	2	2	2	3	3	x 100gm

Long multi-colour sweater

A		3	3	4	4	4	x 100gm
B		3	3	3	4	4	x 100gm
C		3	4	4	4	4	x 100gm
D		3	3	3	4	4	x 100gm

(not photographed)

Short two-colour sweater

A		4	4	4	5	5	x 100gm
B		3	4	4	4	5	x 100gm

(not photographed)

NEEDLES

1 pair 8mm (UK 0) (US 11) needles
1 pair 12mm (US 17) needles

TENSION

8 sts and 12 rows to 10 cm measured over stocking stitch using 12mm (US 17) needles.

Two-colour sweater stripe sequence

Beg with a K row, work in st st as folls:
Rows 1 and 2: Using yarn A.
Rows 3 to 8: Using yarn B.
Rows 9 to 12: Using yarn A.
These 12 rows form stripe sequence.

Multi-colour sweater stripe sequence

Beg with a K row, work in st st as folls:
Rows 1 and 2: Using yarn A.
Rows 3 to 8: Using yarn B.
Rows 9 to 14: Using yarn C.
Rows 15 to 20: Using yarn D.
Rows 21 to 24: Using yarn A.
These 24 rows form stripe sequence.

BACK

Cast on 42 (44: 46: 48: 50) sts using 8mm (US 11) needles and yarn A.
Row 1 (RS): P0 (1: 0: 1: 0), *K2, P2, rep from * to last 2 (3: 2: 3: 2) sts, K2, P0 (1: 0: 1: 0).
Row 2: K0 (1: 0: 1: 0), *P2, K2, rep from * to last 2 (3: 2: 3: 2) sts, P2, K0 (1: 0: 1: 0).

These 2 rows form rib.
Work in rib for a further 4 rows, ending with a WS row.
Change to 12mm (US 17) needles.
Beg with a K row, work in st st in appropriate stripe sequence (see above) as folls:

Long sweater
Cont straight until back measures 57 (58: 58: 59: 59) cm, ending with a WS row.

Short sweater
Cont straight until back measures 35 (36: 36: 37: 37) cm, ending with a WS row.

Both sweaters

Shape armholes
Keeping stripes correct, cast off 3 sts at beg of next 2 rows.
36 (38: 40: 42: 44) sts.
Dec 1 st at each end of next 3 rows.
30 (32: 34: 36: 38) sts.
Cont straight until armhole measures 20 (20: 21: 21: 22) cm, ending with a WS row.

Shape shoulders and back neck
Next row (RS): Cast off 4 (4: 5: 5: 5) sts, K until there are 7 (8: 8: 8: 9) sts on right needle and turn, leaving rem sts on a holder.
Work each side of neck separately.
Cast off 3 sts at beg of next row.
Cast off rem 4 (5: 5: 5: 6) sts.
With RS facing, rejoin yarn to rem sts, cast off centre 8 (8: 8: 10: 10) sts, K to end.
Complete to match first side, reversing shapings.

FRONT

Work as given for back until 8 rows less have been worked than on back to start of shoulder shaping, ending with a WS row.

Shape neck
Next row (RS): K11 (12: 13: 13: 14) and turn, leaving rem sts on a holder.
Work each side of neck separately.
Dec 1 st at neck edge of next 2 rows, then on foll alt row.
8 (9: 10: 10: 11) sts.
Work 3 rows, ending with a WS row.

Shape shoulder
Cast off 4 (4: 5: 5: 5) sts at beg of next row.
Work 1 row.
Cast off rem 4 (5: 5: 5: 6) sts.
With RS facing, rejoin yarn to rem sts, cast off centre 8 (8: 8: 10: 10) sts, K to end.
Complete to match first side, reversing shapings.

SLEEVES (both alike)

Cast on 26 (26: 26: 28: 28) sts using 8mm (US 11) needles and yarn A.

Row 1 (RS): K0 (0: 0: 1: 1), *P2, K2, rep from * to last 2 (2: 2: 3: 3) sts, P2, K0 (0: 0: 1: 1).

Row 2: P0 (0: 0: 1: 1), *K2, P2, rep from * to last 2 (2: 2: 3: 3) sts, K2, P0 (0: 0: 1: 1).

These 2 rows form rib.

Work in rib for a further 4 rows, ending with a WS row.

Change to 12mm (US 17) needles.

Beg with a K row, work in st st in appropriate stripe sequence (see above) as folls:

Inc 1 st at each end of 5th (5th: 3rd: 5th: 3rd) and every foll 12th (12th: 10th: 12th: 10th) row until there are 34 (34: 36: 36: 38) sts.

Cont straight until sleeve measures 46 (46: 47: 47: 47) cm, ending with a WS row.

Shape top

Keeping stripes correct, cast off 3 sts at beg of next 2 rows. 28 (28: 30: 30: 32) sts.

Dec 1 st at each end of next and foll 2 alt rows.

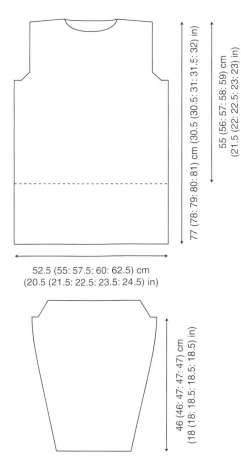

77 (78: 79: 80: 81) cm (30.5 (30.5: 31: 31.5: 32) in)

55 (56: 57: 58: 59) cm (21.5 (22: 22.5: 23: 23) in)

52.5 (55: 57.5: 60: 62.5) cm (20.5 (21.5: 22.5: 23.5: 24.5) in)

46 (46: 47: 47: 47) cm (18 (18: 18.5: 18.5: 18.5) in)

Work 1 row, ending with a WS row.

Cast off rem 22 (22: 24: 24: 26) sts.

MAKING UP

PRESS all pieces as described on the info page.

Join right shoulder seam using back stitch, or mattress st if preferred.

Collar

Long sweater

With RS facing, using 12mm (US 17) needles and yarn A, pick up and knit 10 sts down left side of neck, 8 (8: 8: 10: 10) sts from front, 10 sts up right side of neck, then 14 (14: 14: 16: 16) sts from back. 42 (42: 42: 46: 46) sts.

Beg with a K row, work in st st until collar measures 20cm. Cast off **very loosely**.

Short sweater

With RS facing, using 8mm (US 11) needles and yarn C, pick up and knit 10 sts down left side of neck, 8 (8: 8: 10: 10) sts from front, 10 sts up right side of neck, then 14 (14: 14: 16: 16) sts from back. 42 (42: 42: 46: 46) sts.

Row 1 (WS): K2, *P2, K2, rep from * to end.

Row 2: P2, *K2, P2, rep from * to end.

Rep these 2 rows until collar measures 10cm.

Change to 12mm (US 17) needles.

Cont as set until collar measures 24cm.

Cast off in rib **very loosely**.

Both sweaters

See information page for finishing instructions, setting in sleeves using the shallow set-in method and reversing collar seam for turn-back.

STELLA

KIM HARGREAVES

YARN

Rowan Biggy Print and Big Wool

A	BP	Humbug 254	2	x	100gm
B	BW	Smoky 007	1	x	100gm

NEEDLES

1 pair 10mm (US 15) needles
1 pair 15mm (US 19) needles

TENSION

6 sts and 9½ rows to 10 cm measured over stocking stitch using 15mm (US 19) needles and yarn A.

FINISHED SIZE

Completed bag is 30 cm (11¾ in) wide and 26 cm (10¼ in) deep.

SIDES (make 2)

Cast on 18 sts using 15mm (US 19) needles and yarn A.

Row 1 (RS): Knit.

Row 2: K1, P16, K1.

Rep these 2 rows for 22 cm, ending with a WS row.

Work in garter st for 5 rows, ending with a RS row.

Cast off knitwise (on WS).

HANDLES (make 2)

Cast on 30 sts using 10mm (US 15) needles and yarn B.

Work in garter st for 5 rows.

Cast off knitwise (on WS).

MAKING UP

PRESS as described on the information page.

Join sides along row-end and cast-on edges.

Attach ends of handles inside upper edge, positioning edges of handles approx 5 cm in from side seams.

DESIGN NUMBER 10

DYLAN

KIM HARGREAVES

YARN

	ladies			mens		
	S	M	L	M	L	XL
To fit bust	86	91	97	102	107	112 cm
	34	36	38	40	42	44 in

Rowan Big Wool

| A Artic | 013 | 7 | 8 | 9 | 9 | 10 | 11 x 100gm |
| B Stormy | 011 | 1 | 1 | 1 | 1 | 1 | 1 x 100gm |

NEEDLES

1 pair 12mm (US 17) needles

ZIP – open-ended zip to fit

TENSION

8 sts and 12 rows to 10 cm measured over stocking stitch using 12mm (US 17) needles.

Pattern note: The pattern is written for the 3 ladies sizes, followed by the mens sizes in **bold**. Where only one figure appears this applies to all sizes in that group.

BACK

Cast on 42 (44: 46: **48: 50: 52**) sts using 12mm (US 17) needles and yarn A.
Purl 8 rows, ending with a WS row.

Beg with a K row, cont in st st as folls:
Cont straight until back measures 41 (**43**) cm, ending with a WS row.

Shape raglan armholes
Cast off 3 sts at beg of next 2 rows.
36 (38: 40: **42: 44: 46**) sts.
Dec 1 st at each end of next row.
34 (36: 38: **40: 42: 44**) sts.
Work 1 row, ending with a WS row.
Join in yarn B.
Using yarn B, work 2 rows, dec 1 st at each end of first (first: -: **first: -: -**) of these rows.
32 (34: 38: **38: 42: 44**) sts.
Using yarn A, work 2 rows, dec 1 st at each end of first of these rows.
Using yarn B, work 2 rows, dec 1 st at each end of first of these rows. 28 (30: 34: **34: 38: 40**) sts.
Break off yarn B and cont using yarn A only.
Dec 1 st at each end of next and every foll alt row until 12 (12: 14: **14: 16: 16**) sts rem, then on foll row, ending with a WS row.
Cast off rem 10 (10: 12: **12: 14: 14**) sts.

Pattern note: As row end edges form actual finished front opening edges of garment, it is important these edges are kept neat. Therefore avoid joining in new balls of yarn at these edges.

LEFT FRONT

Cast on 22 (23: 24: **25: 26: 27**) sts using 12mm (US 17) needles and yarn A.
Purl 8 rows, ending with a WS row.
Next row (RS): K to last 2 sts, P2.
Next row: Purl.
These 2 rows set the sts – front opening edge 2 sts worked as P sts on every row with all other sts in st st.
Keeping sts correct as set, cont as folls:
Cont straight until left front matches back to beg of raglan armhole shaping, ending with a WS row.

Shape raglan armhole
Cast off 3 sts at beg of next row.
19 (20: 21: **22: 23: 24**) sts.
Work 1 row. Dec 1 st at raglan armhole edge of next row. 18 (19: 20: **21: 22: 23**) sts.
Work 1 row, ending with a WS row.
Join in yarn B.
Working next 6 rows in stripes (of 2 rows using yarn B, 2 rows using yarn A and 2 rows using yarn B) as given for back and then completing back using yarn A only, cont as folls:

Work 2 (4: 4: **4: 4: 6**) rows, dec 1 st at raglan armhole edge of first (first: 3rd: **first: 3rd: 3rd**) and foll 0 (1: 0: **1: 0: 1**) alt rows.
17 (17: 19: **19: 21: 21**) sts.
Shape front slope
Dec 1 st at both ends of next and every foll alt row until 3 sts rem.
Next row (WS): P3.
Next row: Sl 1, K2tog, psso.
Next row: P1 and fasten off.

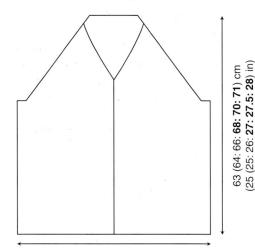

63 (64: 66: **68: 70: 71**) cm
(25 (25: 26: **27: 27.5: 28**) in)

52.5 (55: 57.5: **60: 62.5: 65**) cm
(20.5 (21.5: 22.5: **23.5: 24.5: 25.5**) in)

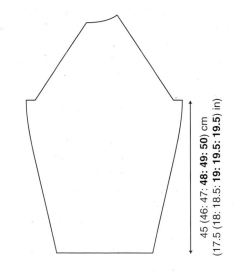

45 (46: 47: **48: 49: 50**) cm
(17.5 (18: 18.5: **19: 19.5: 19.5**) in)

RIGHT FRONT

Cast on 22 (23: 24: **25: 26: 27**) sts using 12mm (US 17) needles and yarn A.

Purl 8 rows, ending with a WS row.

Next row (RS): P2, K to end.

Next row: Purl.

These 2 rows set the sts – front opening edge 2 sts worked as P sts on every row with all other sts in st st.

Keeping sts correct as set, complete to match left front, reversing shapings.

SLEEVES

Cast on 22 (22: 24: **24: 26: 26**) sts using 12mm (US 17) needles and yarn A.

Purl 8 rows, ending with a WS row.

Beg with a K row, cont in st st as folls:

Inc 1 st at each end of 5th (**5th: 5th: 3rd**) and every foll 8th (6th: 6th: **8th: 8th: 6th**) row to 28 (36: 38: **28: 30: 42**) sts, then on every foll 6th (-: -: **6th: 6th: -**) row until there are 34 (-: -: **38: 40: -**) sts.

Cont straight until sleeve measures 45 (46: 47: **48: 49: 50**) cm, ending with a WS row.

Shape raglan

Cast off 3 sts at beg of next 2 rows.

28 (30: 32: **32: 34: 36**) sts.

Dec 1 st at each end of next row.

26 (28: 30: **30: 32: 34**) sts.

Work 1 row, ending with a WS row.

Join in yarn B.

Using yarn B, work 2 rows.

Using yarn A, work 2 rows, dec 1 st at each end of first of these rows. 24 (26: 28: **28: 30: 32**) sts.

Using yarn B, work 2 rows.

Break off yarn B and cont using yarn A only.

Dec 1 st at each end of next and every foll alt row until 12 sts rem.

Work 1 row, ending with a WS row.

Left sleeve only

Dec 1 st at each end of next row. 10 sts.

Cast off 3 sts at beg of next row. 7 sts.

Dec 1 st at beg of next row. 6 sts.

Cast off 3 sts at beg of next row. 3 sts.

Right sleeve only

Cast off 4 sts at beg and dec 1 st at end of next row. 7 sts. Work 1 row.

Cast off 3 sts at beg and dec 1 st at end of next row. 3 sts. Work 1 row.

Both sleeves

Cast off rem 3 sts.

MAKING UP

PRESS all pieces as described on the information page.

Join raglan seams using back stitch, or mattress st if preferred.

Left collar

Cast on 2 sts using 12mm (US 17) needles and yarn A.

Work in garter st for 2 rows, end with a WS row.

Inc 1 st at beg of next and every foll alt row until there are 18 (19: 20: **20: 21: 22**) sts.

Cont straight until left collar, unstretched, fits up left front slope, across top of left sleeve and across to centre back neck.

Cast off **very loosely**.

Right collar

Work to match left collar, reversing shapings.

Join cast-off ends of collars, then sew shaped edge in place, positioning collar cast-on edge at start of front slope shaping. See information page for finishing instructions. Insert zip into front opening.

DESIGN NUMBER 11

LOTTIE

KIM HARGREAVES

YARN

Rowan Big Wool

A Smitten kitten 003	1	x	100gm
B Smoky 007	1	x	100gm

NEEDLES

1 pair 10mm (UK 000) (US 15) needles

DECORATION – one beaded motif (optional)

TENSION

9 sts and 18 rows to 10 cm measured over garter stitch using 10mm (US 15) needles.

FINISHED SIZE

Completed bag is 26.5 cm (10½ in) wide and 30 cm (11¾ in) deep.

SIDES (make 2)

Cast on 20 sts using 10mm (US 15) needles and yarn A.

Row 1 (RS): Inc in first st, K to last st, inc in last st. 22 sts.

Row 2: Knit.

Join in yarn B.

Rows 3 and 4: As rows 1 and 2 but using yarn B. 24 sts.

Rows 5 and 6: Using yarn A, knit.

Rows 7 and 8: Using yarn B, knit.

Rep rows 5 to 8, 10 times more.

Break off yarn A and cont using yarn B only.

Rows 49 to 51: Knit.

Row 52: K7, cast off next 10 sts knitwise (for handle hole), K to end.

Row 53: K7, turn and cast on 10 sts, turn and K rem 7 sts. 24 sts.

Rows 54 to 56: Knit.

Cast off knitwise.

MAKING UP

PRESS as described on the information page.

Join sides along row-end and cast-on edges.

Attach beaded motif as in photograph.

TATE

KIM HARGREAVES

YARN

	XS	S	M	L	XL
To fit bust	81	86	91	97	102 cm
	32	34	36	38	40 in

Rowan Big Wool

| | 11 | 11 | 12 | 13 | 13 | x100gm |

(photographed in Arctic 013)

NEEDLES

1 pair 10mm (UK 000) (US 15) needles

TENSION

8½ sts and 13 rows to 10 cm measured over stocking stitch using 10mm (US 15) needles.

Pattern note: As row end edges of first 30 rows and front opening edges form actual finished edges of garment, it is important these edges are kept neat. Therefore all new balls of yarn should be joined in at side seam or armhole edges of rows.

BACK

Cast on 46 (48: 50: 52: 54) sts using 10mm (US 15) needles.
★★Row 1 (RS): Knit.
Row 2: P to last st, pick up loop lying between needles and place loop on right needle

(**note**: this loop does NOT count as a st), sl last st purlwise.
Row 3: K tog tbl first st and the loop, K to last st, pick up loop lying between needles and place loop on right needle (**note**: this loop does NOT count as a st), sl last st knitwise.
Row 4: P tog first st and the loop, P to last st, pick up loop lying between needles and place loop on right needle, sl last st purlwise.
Last 2 rows set the slip st edging and st st.
Cont as set for a further 26 rows, ending with a WS row.★★
Beg with a K row, cont in st st across all sts as folls:
Work straight until back measures 76 (77: 77: 78: 78) cm, ending with a WS row.
Shape armholes
Cast off 3 sts at beg of next 2 rows.
40 (42: 44: 46: 48) sts.
Dec 1 st at each end of next 3 rows.
34 (36: 38: 40: 42) sts.
Cont straight until armhole measures 25 (25: 26: 26: 27) cm, ending with a WS row.
Shape shoulders and back neck
Cast off 4 (4: 4: 4: 5) sts at beg of next 2 rows.
26 (28: 30: 32: 32) sts.
Next row (RS): Cast off 4 (4: 4: 4: 5) sts, K until there are 6 (7: 8: 8: 7) sts on right needle and turn, leaving rem sts on a holder.
Work each side of neck separately.
Cast off 3 sts at beg of next row.
Cast off rem 3 (4: 5: 5: 4) sts.
With RS facing, rejoin yarn to rem sts, cast off centre 6 (6: 6: 8: 8) sts, K to end.
Complete to match first side, reversing shapings.

LEFT FRONT

Cast on 24 (25: 26: 27: 28) sts using 10mm (US 15) needles.
Work as given for back from ★★ to ★★.
Next row (RS): K to last st, pick up loop lying between needles and place loop on right needle, sl last st knitwise.
Next row: P tog first st and the loop, P to end.
Now working side seam edge st in st st (as set by last 2 rows) and keeping slip st edging at front opening edge correct, cont as folls:
Work straight until left front matches back to beg of armhole shaping, ending with a WS row.
Shape armhole
Cast off 3 sts at beg of next row.
21 (22: 23: 24: 25) sts. Work 1 row.

Dec 1 st at armhole edge of next 2 rows, ending with a WS row. 19 (20: 21: 22: 23) sts.
Shape front slope
Next row (RS): K2tog, K to last 4 sts, K2tog tbl, patt to end.
Working all front slope decreases as set by last row, cont as folls:
Work 3 rows.
Dec 1 st at front slope edge **only** of next and every foll 4th row until 11 (12: 13: 13: 14) sts rem.
Cont straight until left front matches back to start of shoulder shaping, ending with a WS row.
Shape shoulder
Cast off 4 (4: 4: 4: 5) sts at beg of next and foll alt row. Work 1 row. Cast off rem 3 (4: 5: 5: 4) sts.

RIGHT FRONT

Cast on 24 (25: 26: 27: 28) sts using 10mm (US 15) needles.
Work as given for back from ★★ to ★★.
Next row (RS): K tog tbl first st and the loop, K to end.
Next row: P to last st, pick up loop lying between needles and place loop on right needle, sl last st purlwise.
Now working side seam edge st in st st (as set by last 2 rows) and keeping slip st edging at front opening edge correct, cont as folls:
Work straight until right front matches back to beg of armhole shaping, ending with a RS row.
Shape armhole
Cast off 3 sts at beg of next row.
21 (22: 23: 24: 25) sts.
Dec 1 st at armhole edge of next 2 rows, ending with a WS row. 19 (20: 21: 22: 23) sts.
Shape front slope
Next row (RS): Patt 2 sts, K2tog, K to last 2 sts, K2tog.
Working all front slope decreases as set by last row, complete to match left front, reversing shapings.

SLEEVES (both alike)

Cast on 28 (28: 30: 30: 32) sts using 10mm (US 15) needles.
Beg with a K row, work in st st for 14 rows, ending with a WS row.
Cont in st st, shaping sides by inc 1 st at each end of next and every foll 6th row until there are 42 (42: 44: 44: 46) sts.
Cont straight until sleeve measures 45 (45: 46: 46: 46) cm, ending with a WS row.

Shape top

Cast off 3 sts at beg of next 2 rows.
36 (36: 38: 38: 40) sts.
Dec 1 st at each end of next and foll 3 alt rows.
Work 1 row, ending with a WS row.
Cast off rem 28 (28: 30: 30: 32) sts.

MAKING UP

PRESS as described on the information page.
Join both shoulder seams using back stitch, or
mattress st if preferred.

Back neck border

With RS facing and using 10mm (US 15)
needles, pick up and knit 12 (12: 12: 14: 14) sts
from back. Cast off.
See information page for finishing instructions,
leaving side seams open for first 30 rows and
setting in sleeves using the shallow set-in method.

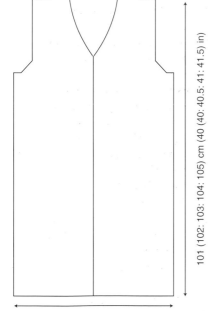

101 (102: 103: 104: 105) cm (40 (40: 40.5: 41: 41.5) in)

54 (56.5: 59: 61: 63.5) cm
(21.5 (22: 23: 24: 25) in)

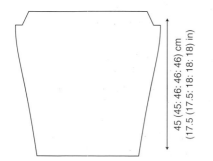

45 (45: 46: 46: 46) cm
(17.5 (17.5: 18: 18: 18) in)

NIK

KIM HARGREAVES

YARN

Striped scarf

Rowan Big Wool

A Whoosh	014	2	x	100gm
B Sherbet Lime	002	2	x	100gm

Plain scarf

Rowan Big Wool and Biggy Print

A BW Arctic	013	4	x	100gm
B BP Swirl	250	1	x	100gm

NEEDLES

1 pair 15mm (US 19) needles

TENSION

7½ sts and 11½ rows to 10 cm measured over
garter stitch using 15mm (US 19) needles.

FINISHED SIZE

Completed scarf is 23 cm (9 in) by 190 cm
(75 in), excluding fringe.

STRIPED SCARF

Cast on 17 sts using 15mm (US 19) needles and
yarn A.
Beg with a RS row, cont in garter st as folls:
Using yarn A, work 2 rows.

Join in yarn B.
Using yarn B, work 2 rows.
Rep these 4 rows until scarf measures 190 cm,
ending after 2 rows using yarn A.
Cast off.

PLAIN SCARF

Cast on 17 sts using 15mm (US 19) needles and
yarn A.
Beg with a RS row, cont in garter st until scarf
measures 190 cm.
Cast off.

MAKING UP

PRESS as described on the information page.

Striped scarf

Cut 24 lengths of yarn A and 16 lengths of yarn
B, each 30 cm long.
Using groups of 4 lengths of yarn, knot fringe
through both ends of scarf as folls: knot yarn A
through each edge st and through centre st, then
use yarn B for a knot midway between knots in
yarn A.

Plain scarf

Cut 18 lengths of yarn B, each 50 cm long.
Form fringe by knotting a length of yarn
through every other st along both ends of scarf.

GWEN

KIM HARGREAVES

YARN

	XS	S	M	L	XL
To fit bust	81	86	91	97	102 cm
	32	34	36	38	40 in

Rowan Big Wool

6 7 7 8 9 x100gm

(photographed in Arctic 013)

NEEDLES

1 pair 12mm (US 17) needles

TENSION

8 sts and 12 rows to 10 cm measured over stocking stitch using 12mm (US 17) needles.

Pattern note: As row end edges form actual finished front opening edges of garment, it is important these edges are kept neat. Therefore avoid joining in new balls of yarn at these edges.

BACK

Cast on 36 (38: 40: 42: 44) sts using 12mm (US 17) needles.
Beg with a K row, cont in st st as folls:
Work 10 rows, ending with a WS row.
Dec 1 st at each end of next and every foll 4th row until 30 (32: 34: 36: 38) sts rem.

Work 7 rows.
Inc 1 st at each end of next and every foll 4th row until there are 36 (38: 40: 42: 44) sts.
Cont straight until back measures 41 (42: 42: 43: 43) cm, ending with a WS row.
Shape armholes
Cast off 2 sts at beg of next 2 rows.
32 (34: 36: 38: 40) sts.
Dec 1 st at each end of next 2 (3: 3: 4: 4) rows.
28 (28: 30: 30: 32) sts.
Cont straight until armhole measures 20 (20: 21: 21: 22) cm, ending with a WS row.
Shape shoulders
Cast off 4 sts at beg of next 2 rows, then 4 (4: 5: 4: 5) sts at beg of foll 2 rows.
Leave rem 12 (12: 12: 14: 14) sts on a holder.

LEFT FRONT

Cast on 18 (19: 20: 21: 22) sts using 12mm (US 17) needles.
Beg with a K row, cont in st st as folls:
Work 10 rows, ending with a WS row.
Dec 1 st at beg of next and every foll 4th row until 15 (16: 17: 18: 19) sts rem.
Work 7 rows. Inc 1 st at beg of next and every foll 4th row until there are 18 (19: 20: 21: 22) sts.
Cont straight until left front matches back to beg of armhole shaping, ending with a WS row.
Shape armhole
Cast off 2 sts at beg of next row.
16 (17: 18: 19: 20) sts.
Work 1 row.
Dec 1 st at armhole edge of next 2 (3: 3: 4: 4) rows.
14 (14: 15: 15: 16) sts.
Cont straight until left front matches back to start of shoulder shaping, ending with a WS row.
Shape shoulder
Cast off 4 sts at beg of next row, then 4 (4: 5: 4: 5) sts at beg of foll alt row.★★
Break yarn and leave rem 6 (6: 6: 7: 7) sts on a holder.

RIGHT FRONT

Cast on 18 (19: 20: 21: 22) sts using 12mm (US 17) needles.
Beg with a K row, cont in st st as folls:
Work 10 rows, ending with a WS row.
Dec 1 st at end of next and every foll 4th row until 15 (16: 17: 18: 19) sts rem.
Complete to match left front to ★★, reversing shapings.

Do NOT break yarn but set this ball aside – it will be used later for collar.

SLEEVES (both alike)

Cast on 20 (20: 22: 22: 24) sts using 12mm (US 17) needles.
Beg with a K row, cont in st st as folls:
Work 14 rows, ending with a WS row.
Inc 1 st at each end of next and every foll 12th row until there are 26 (26: 28: 28: 30) sts.
Cont straight until sleeve measures 45 (45: 46: 46: 46) cm, ending with a WS row.
Shape top
Cast off 2 sts at beg of next 2 rows.
22 (22: 24: 24: 26) sts.
Dec 1 st at each end of next and foll alt row, then on 2 foll 4th rows, then on every foll alt row until 12 sts rem, then on foll row, ending with a WS row.
Cast off rem 10 sts.

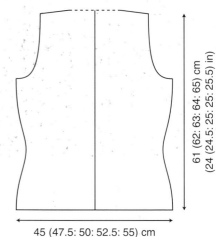

61 (62: 63: 64: 65) cm
(24 (24.5: 25: 25: 25.5) in)

45 (47.5: 50: 52.5: 55) cm
(17.5 (18.5: 19.5: 20.5: 21.5) in)

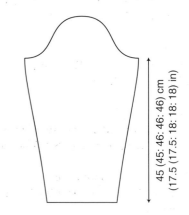

45 (45: 46: 46: 46) cm
(17.5 (17.5: 18: 18: 18) in)

MAKING UP

PRESS all pieces as described on the info page. Join both shoulder seams using back stitch, or mattress st if preferred.

Collar

With RS facing, using 20mm (US 36) needles and ball of yarn set aside with right front, K across 6 (6: 6: 7: 7) sts from right front, 12 (12: 12: 14: 14) sts from back, then 6 (6: 6: 7: 7) sts from left front. 24 (24: 24: 28: 28) sts. Beg with a P row, cont in st st until collar measures 13cm.

Cast off **very loosely**.

See information page for finishing instructions, setting in sleeves using the set-in method. Make two 50cm long crochet or twisted cords and attach to front opening edges level with waist to form ties.

DESIGN NUMBER 15

ZARA

KIM HARGREAVES

YARN

	XS	S	M	L	XL	
To fit bust	81	86	91	97	102	cm
	32	34	36	38	40	in

Rowan Big Wool

	5	5	6	6	7	x100gm

(photographed in White Hot 001)

NEEDLES

1 pair 8mm (UK 0) (US 11) needles
1 pair 12mm (US 17) needles

TENSION

8 sts and 12 rows to 10 cm measured over stocking stitch using 12mm (US 17) needles.

BACK and FRONT (both alike)

Cast on 28 (30: 32: 34: 36) sts using 8mm (US 11) needles.

Row 1 (RS): K1 (0: 1: 0: 1), *P2, K2, rep from * to last 3 (2: 3: 2: 3) sts, P2, K1 (0: 1: 0: 1).
Row 2: P1 (0: 1: 0: 1), *K2, P2, rep from * to last 3 (2: 3: 2: 3) sts, K2, P1 (0: 1: 0: 1).
These 2 rows form rib.
Work in rib for a further 8 rows, inc 1 st at end of last row and ending with a WS row.
29 (31: 33: 35: 37) sts.
Change to 12mm (US 17) needles.
Beg with a K row, work in st st as folls:
Inc 1 st at each end of 7th and foll 8th row.
33 (35: 37: 39: 41) sts.
Cont straight until work measures 29 (30: 30: 31: 31) cm, ending with a WS row.

Shape armholes

Cast off 2 sts at beg of next 2 rows.
29 (31: 33: 35: 37) sts.
Dec 1 st at each end of next 2 (3: 3: 4: 4) rows.
25 (25: 27: 27: 29) sts.
Work a further 10 (9: 11: 10: 12) rows straight, ending with a WS row. Cast off.

SLEEVES (both alike)

Cast on 21 (21: 21: 23: 23) sts using 12mm (US 17) needles.
Beg with a K row, work in st st as folls:
Inc 1 st at each end of 21st (21st: 15th: 21st: 15th) and every foll 16th row until there are 25 (25: 27: 27: 29) sts.
Cont straight until sleeve measures 46 (46: 47: 47: 47) cm, ending with a WS row.

Shape top

Cast off 2 sts at beg of next 2 rows.
21 (21: 23: 23: 25) sts.
Dec 1 st at each end of next and every foll alt row until 9 sts rem, then on foll row, ending with a WS row. Cast off rem 7 sts.

MAKING UP

PRESS all pieces as described on the info page. Matching cast-off edges of sleeve tops to cast-off edges of back and front, sew sleeves into armholes, leaving left back armhole seam open.

Collar

With RS facing and using 8mm (US 11) needles, pick up and knit 5 sts from left sleeve, 24 (24: 26: 26: 28) sts from front, 5 sts from right sleeve, then 24 (24: 26: 26: 28) sts from back.
58 (58: 62: 62: 66) sts.
Row 1 (WS): P2, *K2, P2, rep from * to end.
Row 2: K2, *P2, K2, rep from * to end.
These 2 rows form rib.
Cont in rib until collar measures 8 cm.
Change to 12mm (US 17) needles.
Cont in rib until collar measures 16 cm.
Cast off in rib **very loosely**.
Join left back armhole and collar seam, reversing collar seam for turn-back. See information page for finishing instructions.

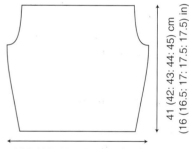

41 (42: 43: 44: 45) cm
(16 (16.5: 17: 17.5: 17.5) in)

41.5 (44: 46.5: 49: 51.5) cm
(16.5 (17.5: 18.5: 19.5: 20.5) in)

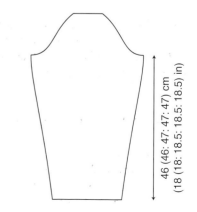

46 (46: 47: 47: 47) cm
(18 (18: 18.5: 18.5: 18.5) in)

MINI

KIM HARGREAVES

YARN

Rowan Big Wool

		S	M	L		
Plain hat		1	1	1	x	100gm
(not photographed)						
Hat with contrast band						
A Shocking	009	1	1	1	x	100gm
B Whoosh	014	1	1	1	x	100gm
Striped hat						
A Pip	015	1	1	1	x	100gm
B Sherbet Lime	002	1	1	1	x	100gm

NEEDLES

1 pair 10mm (UK 000) (US 15) needles

TENSION

8½ sts and 13 rows to 10 cm measured over
stocking stitch using 10mm (US 15) needles.

PLAIN HAT

Cast on 37 (41: 45) sts using 10mm (US 15)
needles.
Beg with a K row, cont in st st as folls:
Work 20 rows, ending with a WS row.
Shape top
Small and large sizes only
Next row (RS): ★K7 (-: 9), K2tog, rep from ★

to last st, K1. 33 (-: 41) sts.
Work 1 row.
Medium and large sizes only
Next row (RS): (K7, K3tog) 4 times, K1.
– (33: 33) sts.
Work 1 row.
All sizes
Next row: (K5, K3tog) 4 times, K1. 25 sts.
Work 1 row.
Next row: (K3, K3tog) 4 times, K1. 17 sts.
Next row: P1, (P2tog) 8 times.
Break yarn and thread through rem 9 sts.
Pull up tight and fasten off securely.

HAT WITH CONTRAST BAND
Work as given for plain hat (above) but casting
on and working first 8 rows using yarn A and
then completing hat using yarn B.

STRIPED HAT
Work as given for plain hat (above) but casting on
and working first 6 rows using yarn A, working
(2 rows using yarn B, then 2 rows using yarn A)
3 times and then completing hat using yarn B.

MAKING UP
PRESS as described on the information page.

GABBY

KIM HARGREAVES

YARN

	XS	S	M	L	XL	
To fit bust	81	86	91	97	102	cm
	32	34	36	38	40	in
Rowan Big Wool						
	10	10	11	11	12	x100gm

(photographed in Cheeky 010)

NEEDLES

1 pair 12mm (US 17) needles

TENSION

8 sts and 12 rows to 10 cm measured over
stocking stitch using 12mm (US 17) needles.

SPECIAL ABBREVIATION

wrap next st = slip next st to right needle, bring
yarn to front of work between needles and then
slip same st back onto left needle. (When working
back across sts, take wrapped loop and st it wraps
tog as one st.)

BACK

Cast on 43 (45: 47: 49: 51) sts using 12mm (US 17)
needles. Beg with a K row, work in st st as folls:
Cont straight until back measures 40 (41: 41: 42:
42) cm, ending with a WS row.

Shape armholes

Cast off 3 sts at beg of next 2 rows.

37 (39: 41: 43: 45) sts.

Dec 1 st at each end of next 3 rows.

31 (33: 35: 37: 39) sts.

Cont straight until armhole measures 25 (25: 26: 26: 27) cm, ending with a WS row.

Shape shoulders and back neck

Next row (RS): Cast off 4 (4: 5: 5: 5) sts, K until there are 6 (7: 7: 7: 8) sts on right needle and turn, leaving rem sts on a holder.

Work each side of neck separately.

Cast off 3 sts at beg of next row.

Cast off rem 3 (4: 4: 4: 5) sts.

With RS facing, rejoin yarn to rem sts, cast off centre 11 (11: 11: 13: 13) sts, K to end.

Complete to match first side, reversing shapings.

FRONT

Work as given for back until 8 rows less have been worked than on back to start of shoulder shaping, ending with a WS row.

Shape neck

Next row (RS): K10 (11: 12: 12: 13) and turn, leaving rem sts on a holder.

Work each side of neck separately.

Dec 1 st at neck edge of next 2 rows, then on foll alt row.

7 (8: 9: 9: 10) sts.

Work 3 rows, ending with a WS row.

Shape shoulder

Cast off 4 (4: 5: 5: 5) sts at beg of next row.

Work 1 row.

Cast off rem 3 (4: 4: 4: 5) sts.

With RS facing, rejoin yarn to rem sts, cast off centre 11 (11: 11: 13: 13) sts, K to end.

Complete to match first side, reversing shapings.

SLEEVES (both alike)

Cast on 29 (29: 29: 31: 31) sts using 12mm (US 17) needles.

Purl 8 rows, ending with a WS row.

Beg with a K row, work in st st as folls:

Inc 1 st at each end of 3rd (3rd: next: 3rd: next) and every foll 10th (10th: 8th: 10th: 8th) row to 37 (37: 41: 41: 43) sts, then on every foll 8th (8th: -: 8th: -) row until there are 39 (39: -: 41: -) sts.

Cont straight until sleeve measures 45 (45: 46: 46: 46) cm, ending with a WS row.

Shape top

Cast off 3 sts at beg of next 2 rows.

33 (33: 35: 35: 37) sts.

Dec 1 st at each end of next and foll 3 alt rows.

Work 1 row, ending with a WS row.

Cast off rem 25 (25: 27: 27: 29) sts.

MAKING UP

PRESS all pieces as described on the information page.

Join shoulder seams using back stitch, or mattress st if preferred.

Collar

Cast on 26 sts using 12mm (US 17) needles.

Work in garter st for 6 rows.

Row 7 (RS): K10, wrap next st and turn.

Row 8: K10.

Row 9: K15, wrap next st and turn.

Row 10: K15.

Work in garter st for a further 4 rows.

Rep last 14 rows 10 (10: 10: 11: 11) times more.

Cast off.

Join cast-on and cast-off ends of collar, then sew shorter edge to neck edge, positioning collar seam at centre back.

See information page for finishing instructions, setting in sleeves using the shallow set-in method and reversing collar seam for turn-back.

Hem border

Cast on 9 sts using 12mm (US 17) needles.

Row 1 (RS): K2, (yfwd, K2tog) twice, yfwd, K3.

Row 2 and every foll alt row: Knit.

Row 3: K2, (yfwd, K2tog) twice, yfwd, K4.

Row 5: K2, (yfwd, K2tog) twice, yfwd, K5.

Row 7: K2, (yfwd, K2tog) twice, yfwd, K6.

Row 9: K2, (yfwd, K2tog) twice, yfwd, K7.

Row 11: K2, (yfwd, K2tog) twice, yfwd, K8.

Row 12: Cast off 6 sts, K to end. 9 sts.

Rep these 12 rows until hem border fits around entire lower edge of garment, ending with row 12.

Cast off.

Join ends of hem border, then sew straight edge to lower edge of garment, positioning border seam at left side seam.

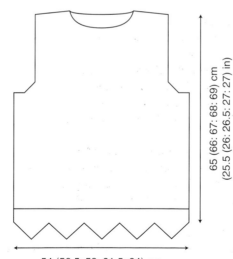

65 (66: 67: 68: 69) cm
(25.5 (26: 26.5: 27: 27) in)

54 (56.5: 59: 61.5: 64) cm
(21.5 (22: 23: 24: 25) in)

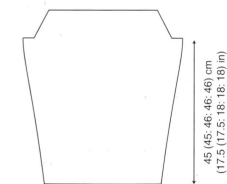

45 (45: 46: 46: 46) cm
(17.5 (17.5: 18: 18: 18) in)

EVA

KIM HARGREAVES

YARN
Rowan Biggy Print
4   x   100gm
(photographed in Joker 253)

NEEDLES
1 pair 20mm (US 36) needles

RIBBONS – approx 40 x 40 cm lengths of double-sided satin ribbon in assorted widths and shades to match knitting yarn

TENSION
5½ sts and 7 rows to 10 cm measured over stocking stitch using 20mm (US 36) needles.

FINISHED SIZE
Completed scarf is 22 cm (8½ in) by 180 cm (71 in), excluding fringe.

SCARF
Cast on 12 sts using 20mm (US 36) needles.
Rows 1 to 4: Knit.
Row 5: K to end, winding yarn twice round needle for each st.

Continued on page 53

MADGE

KIM HARGREAVES

YARN
To fit average sized adult head
Rowan Big Wool
              1   x   100gm
(photographed in White Hot 001)

NEEDLES
1 pair 10mm (UK 000) (US 15) needles

TENSION
8½ sts and 13 rows to 10 cm measured over stocking stitch using 10mm (US 15) needles.

HAT
Cast on 41 sts using 10mm (US 15) needles.
Purl 8 rows, ending with a WS row.
Cont in moss st as folls:
Row 1 (RS): K1, ★P1, K1, rep from ★ to end.
Row 2: As row 1.
These 2 rows form moss st.
Work in moss st for a further 14 rows, ending with a WS row.
Shape top
Row 1 (RS): (Moss st 7 sts, P3tog) 4 times, K1. 33 sts.

Continued on page 53

CARRIE

KIM HARGREAVES

YARN
To fit average sized adult head
Rowan Big Wool
              1   x   100gm
(photographed in Sugar Spun 016)

NEEDLES
1 pair 10mm (UK 000) (US 15) needles

TENSION
8½ sts and 13 rows to 10 cm measured over stocking stitch using 10mm (US 15) needles.

SPECIAL ABBREVIATION
wrap next st = slip next st, bring yarn to front (WS) of work between needles and slip same st back onto left needle, then take yarn back to back (RS) of work. (When working back across sts, take wrapped loop and st it wraps tog as one st.)

HAT
Cast on 21 sts using 10mm (US 15) needles.
Row 1 to 3: Knit.
Row 4 (WS): K13, wrap next st and turn.
Row 5: K13.

Continued on page 53

PATTY

KIM HARGREAVES

YARN
To fit average sized adult head
Rowan Biggy Print
        1   x   100gm
(photographed in Dull 240)

NEEDLES
1 pair 20mm (US 36) needles

TENSION
$4\frac{1}{2}$ sts and 8 rows to 10 cm measured over pattern using 20mm (US 36) needles.

HAT
Cast on 22 sts using 20mm (US 36) needles.
Row 1 (RS): K1, ★yfwd, sl 1, K1, psso, rep from ★ to last st, K1.
Row 2: As row 1.
These 2 rows form patt.
Work in patt for a further 10 rows.
Shape top
Row 1 (RS): K1, ★sl 1, K1, psso, rep from ★ to last st, K1. 12 sts.
Row 2: (P2tog) 6 times.
Break yarn and thread through rem 6 sts.

Continued on page 53

GUY

KIM HARGREAVES

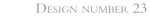

YARN
Rowan Big Wool
A Stormy   011   3   x   100gm
B Black   008   1   x   100gm

NEEDLES
1 pair 15mm (US 19) needles

TENSION
$7\frac{1}{2}$ sts and $10\frac{1}{2}$ rows to 10 cm measured over moss stitch using 15mm (US 19) needles.

FINISHED SIZE
Completed scarf is 23 cm (9 in) by 190 cm (75 in), excluding fringe.

SCARF
Cast on 17 sts using 15mm (US 19) needles and yarn A.
Work in garter st for 6 rows, end with a WS row.
Row 7 (RS): K1, ★P1, K1, rep from ★ to end.
Row 8: As row 7.
Last 2 rows form moss st.
Cont in moss st until scarf measures 185 cm, ending with a WS row.

Continued on page 53

KYLE

KIM HARGREAVES

YARN
Rowan Biggy Print
        5   x   100gm
(photographed in Dull 240)

NEEDLES
1 pair 20mm (US 36) needles

TENSION
$4\frac{1}{2}$ sts and 8 rows to 10 cm measured over pattern using 20mm (US 36) needles.

FINISHED SIZE
Completed scarf is 31 cm ($12\frac{1}{4}$ in) by 180 cm (71 in), excluding fringe.

SCARF
Cast on 14 sts using 20mm (US 36) needles.
Row 1 (RS): K1, ★yfwd, sl 1, K1, psso, rep from ★ to last st, K1.
Row 2: As row 1.
These 2 rows form patt.
Cont in patt until scarf measures 180 cm.
Cast off.

Continued on page 53

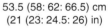

Sharleen

Kim Hargreaves

YARN

	XS-S	S-M	M-L	L-XL	
To fit bust	81–86	86–91	91–97	97–102	cm
	32–34	34–36	36–38	38–40	in

Rowan Biggy Print

| | 10 | 11 | 12 | 13 | x 100gm |

(photographed in Swirl 250)

NEEDLES

1 pair 20mm (US 36) needles

TENSION

4½ sts and 8 rows to 10 cm measured over pattern using 20mm (US 36) needles.

BACK

Cast on 24 (26: 28: 30) sts using 20mm (US 36) needles.

Row 1 (RS): K1, *yfwd, sl 1, K1, psso, rep from * to last st, K1.

Row 2: As row 1.

These 2 rows form patt.

Cont in patt until back measures 46 cm, ending with a WS row.

Shape armholes

Keeping patt correct, cast off 3 sts at beg of next 2 rows. 18 (20: 22: 24) sts.

Cont straight until armhole measures 24 (25: 26: 27) cm, ending with a WS row.

Shape shoulders and back neck

Next row (RS): Cast off 2 (3: 3: 3) sts, patt until there are 5 (5: 5: 6) sts on right needle and turn, leaving rem sts on a holder.

Work each side of neck separately.

Cast off 2 sts at beg of next row.

Cast off rem 3 (3: 3: 4) sts.

With RS facing, rejoin yarn to rem sts, cast off centre 4 (4: 6: 6) sts, patt to end.

Complete to match first side, reversing shapings.

FRONT

Work as given for back until 6 rows less have been worked than on back to start of shoulder shaping, ending with a WS row.

Shape neck

Next row (RS): Patt 7 (8: 8: 9) sts and turn, leaving rem sts on a holder.

Work each side of neck separately.

Dec 1 st at neck edge of next 2 rows.

5 (6: 6: 7) sts.

Work 3 rows, ending with a WS row.

Shape shoulder

Cast off 2 (3: 3: 3) sts at beg of next row.

Work 1 row.

Cast off rem 3 (3: 3: 4) sts.

With RS facing, rejoin yarn to rem sts, cast off centre 4 (4: 6: 6) sts, patt to end.

Complete to match first side, reversing shapings.

SLEEVES (both alike)

Cast on 16 (16: 18: 18) sts using 20mm (US 36) needles.

Work in patt as given for back for 10 rows, ending with a WS row.

Inc 1 st at each end of next and every foll 10th row until there are 22 (22: 24: 24) sts, taking inc sts into patt.

Cont straight until sleeve measures 50 (50: 51: 51) cm, ending with a WS row.

Cast off **very loosely**.

MAKING UP

PRESS all pieces as described on the information page.

Join right shoulder seam using back stitch, or mattress st if preferred.

Collar

With RS facing and using 20mm (US 36) needles,

pick up and knit 8 sts down left side of neck, 4 (4: 6: 6) sts from front, 8 sts up right side of neck, then 8 (8: 10: 10) sts from back.

28 (28: 32: 32) sts.

Work in patt as given for back for 20cm.

Cast off **very loosely**.

See information page for finishing instructions, setting in sleeves using the square set-in method.

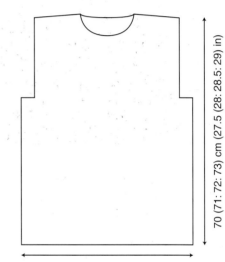

53.5 (58: 62: 66.5) cm
(21 (23: 24.5: 26) in)

70 (71: 72: 73) cm (27.5 (28: 28.5: 29) in)

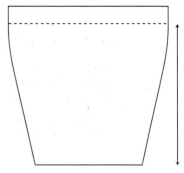

44 (44: 45: 45) cm (17.5 in)

GINA

KIM HARGREAVES

YARN

	XS	S	M	L	XL
To fit bust	81	86	91	97	102 cm
	32	34	36	38	40 in

Rowan Biggy Print

11	12	13	14	15	x100gm

(photographed in Thunder 252)

NEEDLES

1 pair 20mm (US 36) needles

TENSION

5½ sts and 7 rows to 10 cm measured over stocking stitch using 20mm (US 36) needles.

Pattern note: As row end edges of first 14 rows and front opening edges form actual finished edges of garment, it is important these edges are kept neat. Therefore all new balls of yarn should be joined in at side seam or armhole edges of rows.

BACK

Cast on 29 (31: 33: 35: 37) sts using 20mm (US 36) needles.
★★Row 1 (RS): Knit.

Row 2: P to last st, pick up loop lying between needles and place loop on right needle (**note**: this loop does NOT count as a st), sl last st purlwise.
Row 3: K tog tbl first st and the loop, K to last st, pick up loop lying between needles and place loop on right needle (**note**: this loop does NOT count as a st), sl last st knitwise.
Row 4: P tog first st and the loop, P to last st, pick up loop lying between needles and place loop on right needle, sl last st purlwise.
Last 2 rows set the slip st edging and st st.
Cont as set for a further 10 rows, ending with a WS row.★★★
Beg with a K row, now cont in st st over all sts as folls:
Work straight until back measures 59 (60: 60: 61: 61) cm, ending with a WS row.
Shape armholes
Cast off 2 sts at beg of next 2 rows.
25 (27: 29: 31: 33) sts.
Dec 1 st at each end of next 2 rows.
21 (23: 25: 27: 29) sts.
Cont straight until armhole measures 25 (25: 26: 26: 27) cm, ending with a WS row.
Shape shoulders
Cast off 3 (3: 4: 4: 4) sts at beg of next 2 rows, then 3 (4: 4: 4: 5) sts at beg of foll 2 rows.
Cast off rem 9 (9: 9: 11: 11) sts.

LEFT FRONT

Cast on 15 (16: 17: 18: 19) sts using 20mm (US 36) needles.
Work as given for back from ★★ to ★★★.
Next row (RS): K to last st, pick up loop lying between needles and place loop on right needle, sl last st knitwise.
Next row: P tog first st and the loop, P to end.
Now working side seam edge st in st st (as set by last 2 rows) and keeping slip st edging at front opening edge correct, cont as folls:
Work straight until left front matches back to beg of armhole shaping, ending with a WS row.
Shape armhole
Cast off 2 sts at beg of next row.
13 (14: 15: 16: 17) sts.
Work 1 row.
Dec 1 st at armhole edge of next 2 rows.
11 (12: 13: 14: 15) sts.
Work 2 rows, ending with a WS row.

Shape front slope
Next row (RS): K to last 4 sts, K2tog tbl, patt to end.
Working all front slope decreases as set by last row, cont as folls:
Work 1 row.
Dec 1 st at front slope edge of next and foll 3 (3: 3: 4: 4) alt rows.
6 (7: 8: 8: 9) sts.
Cont straight until left front matches back to start of shoulder shaping, ending with a WS row.
Shape shoulder
Cast off 3 (3: 4: 4: 4) sts at beg of next row.
Work 1 row.
Cast off rem 3 (4: 4: 4: 5) sts.

RIGHT FRONT

Cast on 15 (16: 17: 18: 19) sts using 20mm (US 36) needles.
Work as given for back from ★★ to ★★★.
Next row (RS): K tog tbl first st and the loop, K to end.
Next row: P to last st, pick up loop lying between needles and place loop on right needle, sl last st purlwise.
Complete to match left front, reversing shapings and working front slope decrease rows as folls:
Next row (RS): Patt 2 sts, K2tog, K to end.

SLEEVES (both alike)

Cast on 19 (19: 21: 21: 21) sts using 20mm (US 36) needles.
Beg with a K row, work in st st for 8 (8: 8: 8: 6) rows.
Cont in st st, shaping sides by inc 1 st at each end of next and every foll 6th (6th: 6th: 6th: 4th) row to 27 (27: 29: 29: 27) sts, then on every foll – (–: –: –: 6th) row until there are – (–: –: –: 31) sts.
Cont straight until sleeve measures 45 (45: 46: 46: 46) cm, ending with a WS row.
Shape top
Cast off 2 sts at beg of next 2 rows.
23 (23: 25: 25: 27) sts.
Dec 1 st at each end of next row.
Work 1 row, ending with a WS row.
Cast off rem 21 (21: 23: 23: 25) sts.

MAKING UP

PRESS as described on the information page.
Join both shoulder seams using back stitch, or mattress st if preferred.

Back neck border
With RS facing and using 20mm (US 36) needles, pick up and knit 9 (9: 9: 11: 11) sts from back.
Cast off evenly (on WS).
See information page for finishing instructions, leaving side seams open for first 14 rows and setting in sleeves using the shallow set-in method.

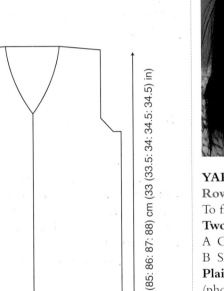

52.5 (56.5: 60: 63.5: 67.5) cm
(20.5 (22: 23.5: 25: 26.5) in)

84 (85: 86: 87: 88) cm (33 (33.5: 34: 34.5: 34.5) in)

45 (45: 46: 46: 46) cm
(17.5 (17.5: 18: 18: 18) in)

ASH

KIM HARGREAVES

YARN
Rowan Big Wool
To fit average sized adult hand
Two colour mittens

A Cheeky	010	1	x	100gm
B Shocking	009	1	x	100gm
Plain mittens		1	x	100gm

(photographed in White Hot 001)

NEEDLES
1 pair 10mm (UK 000) (US 15) needles

TENSION
8½ sts and 13 rows to 10 cm measured over stocking stitch using 10mm (US 15) needles.

Two colour mittens
RIGHT MITTEN
Cast on 20 sts using 10mm (US 15) needles and yarn A.
Beg with a K row, cont in st st as folls:
Work 6 rows.
Break off yarn A and join in yarn B.
Work a further 10 rows, ending with a WS row.★
Shape for thumb
Next row (RS): K15 and turn.
★★Next row: Cast on and P 5 sts, P5 and turn.

Work 6 rows on these 10 sts.
Break yarn and thread through rem 10 sts. Pull up tight and fasten off securely. Join thumb seam.
With RS facing, rejoin yarn at base of thumb, pick up and knit 5 sts from base of thumb, K to end. 20 sts. Work a further 9 rows over all sts.
Break off yarn B and join in yarn A.
Work a further 6 rows, ending with a WS row.
Next row (RS): (K2tog) 10 times.
Break yarn and thread through rem 10 sts. Pull up tight and fasten off securely. Join side seam.

LEFT MITTEN
Work as given for right mitten to ★.
Shape for thumb
Next row (RS): K10 and turn.
Complete as for right mitten from ★★.

Plain mittens
Work as given for two colour mittens (above), but using same colour throughout.

MAKING UP
PRESS as described on the information page.
If desired, make a 150 cm long twisted or crochet cord and attach one end to base of side seam of each mitten.

GUY

Continued from page 49
Work in garter st for 7 rows.
Cast off knitwise (on WS).

MAKING UP
PRESS as described on the information page.
Cut 40 lengths of yarn B, each 20 cm long.
Using groups of 4 lengths of yarn, knot fringe
through both ends of scarf as folls: make one
knot on each edge st and through centre st, then
make a knot midway between previous knots.

EVA

Continued from page 48
Row 6: K to end, letting extra loops drop.
These 6 rows form patt.
Cont in patt until scarf measures approx 180 cm,
ending after patt row 4.
Knit 1 row, then cast off knitwise on WS.

MAKING UP
PRESS as described on the information page.
Knot lengths of ribbon through both ends of
scarf to form fringe.

CARRIE

Continued from page 48
Row 6: K16, wrap next st and turn.
Row 7: K16.
Rows 8 and 9: As rows 4 and 5.
Row 10: Knit.
Rep these 10 rows 6 times more.
Cast off.

MAKING UP
PRESS as described on the information page.
Join cast-on and cast-off edges to form back seam.
Run gathering thread around shorter row end
edge, pull up tight and fasten off securely. Make
8 cm diameter pompom and attach to top of hat.

PATTY

Continued from page 49
Pull up tight and fasten off securely.

MAKING UP
PRESS as described on the information page.
Join back seam.

MADGE

Continued from page 48
Work 1 row.
Row 3: (Moss st 5 sts, P3tog) 4 times, K1. 25 sts.
Work 1 row.
Row 5: (Moss st 3 sts, P3tog) 4 times, K1. 17 sts.
Row 6: P1, (P2tog) 8 times.
Break yarn and thread through rem 9 sts. Pull up
tight and fasten off securely.

MAKING UP
PRESS as described on the information page.
Join back seam.

KYLE

Continued from page 49
MAKING UP
PRESS as described on the information page.
Cut 42 lengths of yarn, each 40 cm long. Using
groups of 3 lengths of yarn, knot fringe through
both ends of scarf as folls: make one knot on
each edge st and through centre st, then make 2
knots evenly spaced between previous knots.

Photographer Joey Toller • Stylist Kim Hargreaves • Hair & Make-up Annabel Hobbs • Models Zoe, Alexandra & Alistair

INFORMATION PAGE

TENSION

Obtaining the correct tension is perhaps the single factor which can make the difference between a successful garment and a disastrous one. It controls both the shape and size of an article, so **any** variation, can distort the finished look of the garment. We recommend that you knit a square in pattern and/or stocking stitch of perhaps 5 more stitches and rows than those given in the tension note. Press the finished square under a damp cloth and mark out the central 10cm square. If you have too many stitches to 10cm try again using thicker needles, if you have too few stitches to 10cm try again using finer needles.

SIZING AND SIZE DIAGRAM NOTE

The instructions are given for the smallest size. Where they vary, work the figures in brackets for the larger sizes. **One set of figures refers to all sizes.** Included with every pattern in this magazine is a '**size diagram**', the purpose of which is to enable you to accurately achieve a perfect fitting garment without the need for worry during knitting. The size diagram shows the finished width of the garment at the under-arm point, and it is this measurement that the knitter should choose first. Next look at the corresponding length for that size; if you are not happy with the total length which we recommend, adjust your own garment before beginning your armhole shaping - any adjustment after this point will mean that your sleeve will not fit into your garment easily - don't forget to take your adjustment into account if there is any side seam shaping. Finally, look at the sleeve length; the size diagram shows the finished sleeve measurement, taking into account any top-arm insertion length. Measure your body between the centre of your neck and your wrist, this measurement should correspond to half the garment width plus the sleeve length. Again, your sleeve length may be adjusted, but remember to take into consideration your sleeve increases if you do adjust the length - you must increase more frequently than the pattern states to shorten your sleeve, less frequently to lengthen it.

FINISHING INSTRUCTIONS

After working for hours knitting a garment, it seems a great pity that many garments are spoiled because such little care is taken in the pressing and finishing process.

PRESSING

Darn in all ends neatly along the selvage edge or a colour join, as appropriate. Block out each piece of knitting using pins and gently press each piece, omitting the ribs, using a warm iron over a damp cloth. **Tip**: Take special care to press the edges, as this will make sewing up both easier and neater.

STITCHING

When stitching the pieces together, remember to match areas of colour and texture very carefully where they meet.
Use a seam stitch such as back stitch or mattress stitch for all main knitting seams, and join all ribs and neckband with a flat seam unless otherwise stated.

CONSTRUCTION

Having completed the pattern instructions, join left shoulder and neckband seams as detailed above. Sew the top of the sleeve to the body of the garment using the method detailed in the pattern, referring to the appropriate guide:

Square set-in sleeves: Set sleeve head into armhole, the straight sides at top of sleeve to form a neat right-angle to cast-off sts at armhole on back and front.

Shallow set-in sleeves: Join cast-off sts at beg of armhole shaping to cast-off sts at start of sleeve-head shaping. Sew sleeve head into armhole, easing in shapings.

Set-in sleeves: Set in sleeve, easing sleeve head into armhole.

JOIN SIDE AND SLEEVE SEAMS.

Slip stitch pocket edgings and linings into place. Sew on buttons to correspond with buttonholes. After sewing up, press seams and hems. Ribbed welts and neckbands and any areas of garter stitch should not be pressed.

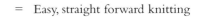